JOBS IN ENGINEERING

By Bethany Latham

KidHaven PUBLISHING

Published in 2026 by
KidHaven Publishing, an Imprint of
Greenhaven Publishing, LLC
2544 Clinton St., Buffalo, NY 14224

Written by: Bethany Latham
Edited by: Rebecca Phillips-Bartlett
Designed by: Rob Delph

All facts, statistics, web addresses, and URLs in this book were verified as valid and accurate at time of writing. No responsibility for any changes to external websites or references can be accepted by either the author or publisher.

Cataloging-in-Publication Data
Names: Latham, Bethany.
Title: Jobs in engineering / Bethany Latham.
Description: Buffalo, NY : KidHaven Publishing, 2026. | Series: STEAM job? Dream job! | Includes glossary and index.
Identifiers: ISBN 9781534552159 (pbk.) | ISBN 9781534552166 (library bound) | ISBN 9781534552173 (ebook)
Subjects: LCSH: Engineers--Vocational guidance--Juvenile literature. | Engineers--Juvenile literature.
Classification: LCC TA157.L384 2026 | DDC 620.0023--dc23

Printed in China

CPSIA compliance information: Batch #QW26KH: For further information contact Greenhaven Publishing LLC at 1-844-317-7404.

IMAGE CREDITS

Images courtesy of Shutterstock.com, unless otherwise stated.

Cover – Gorodenkoff. 2–3 – grmarc, kelvn, NewJadsada. 4–5 – Amnaj Khetsamtip, Gorodenkoff, kittirat roekburi, Lysenko Andrii, APChanel, Macrovector, curiosity, riabchevskii. 6–7 – Quality Stock Arts, Kathy Kate. 8–9 – benixs, KlingSup, Anditya Creative. 10–11 – Gorodenkoff, shurkin_son, Andrey Sayfutdinov, grmarc, Studio_G. 12–13 – NewJadsada, Hryshchyshen Serhii, Iconsanta. 14–15 – Dan76, Gorodenkoff, Sabelskaya, curiosity. 16–17 – Juice Flair, Sebastian stocking, Macrovector. 18–19 – kittirat roekburi. 20–21 – Friends Stock, Gorodenkoff, ivector. 22–23 – PeopleImages.com - Yuri A, Dusan Petkovic, riabchevskii, Anditya Creative. 24 – Iconsanta, Macrovector. Vectors used throughout – Pavlo S, YamabikaY.

CONTENTS

Words that look like **this** can be found in the glossary on page 24.

ALL ABOUT STEAM

Have you ever thought about having a STEAM **career** when you grow up? STEAM careers use science, technology, engineering, the arts, and math. There are many different things you can do with STEAM skills.

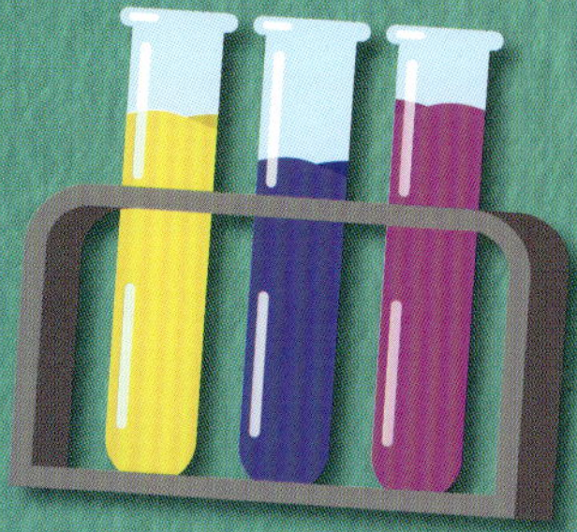

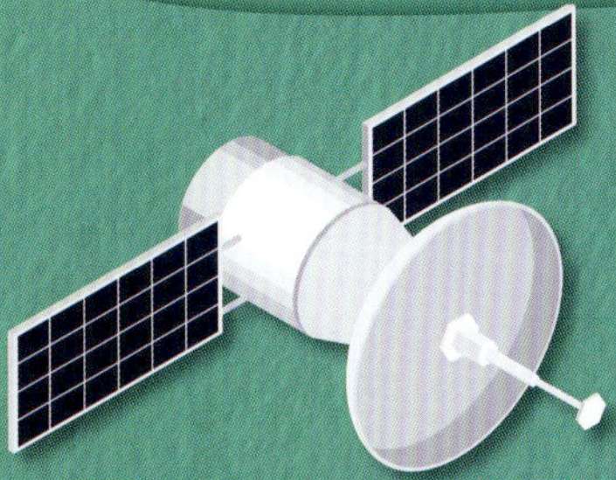

You could work in many different fields with a STEAM job, including building, medicine, and television. STEAM subjects link together. The skills you learn in one subject can help you in another.

ALL ABOUT ENGINEERING

Engineering means designing, making, and using machines, tools, and buildings. Engineering is all about problem solving. Engineers design and build things to help solve human and **environmental** problems.

THE WORD "ENGINEER" WAS FIRST USED AROUND THE 1300S.

There are many different areas of engineering. Engineers can work in medicine, farming, city planning, vehicle repair, and more. Engineers are needed everywhere! Different engineering jobs need different skills and training.

MECHANICAL ENGINEER

Mechanical engineers design and build mechanical **devices**. These devices include engines, tools, and other machines. Mechanical engineers solve problems. They make devices for specific needs. They also make machines easier to use.

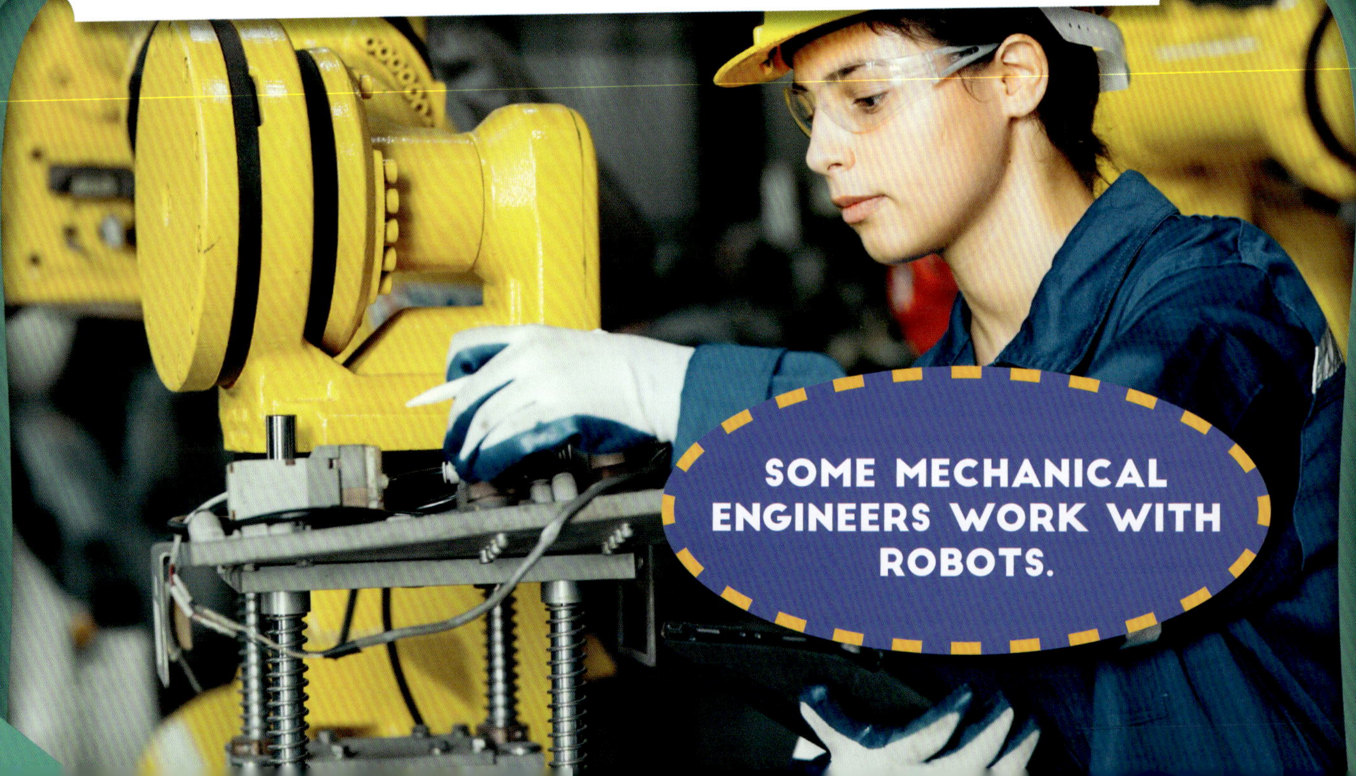

SOME MECHANICAL ENGINEERS WORK WITH ROBOTS.

Mechanical engineers often work on a project from beginning to end. They research, design, build, and test the devices they create. Mechanical engineers need to understand how each step in a process works. They need good planning skills.

BIOMEDICAL ENGINEER

Biomedical engineers design and build **equipment** and technology that helps sick and hurt people. They create **prosthetic limbs** and make machines to treat and test for illnesses. Biomedical engineers often work in research laboratories.

Some biomedical engineers are called clinical engineers. They work in hospitals to make sure the medical machines are working. Biomedical engineers need to know about technology and medicine. They study for many years.

SOLAR ENGINEER

Solar engineers help the environment by designing and building solar panels to collect solar energy. Solar energy comes from the sun. Solar engineers also fix solar technology if it breaks.

SOLAR ENERGY IS RENEWABLE, WHICH MEANS IT WILL NOT RUN OUT.

Solar engineers work to keep solar technology **affordable**. This allows more people to use solar power. Solar engineers need good math, technology, and science skills. They study for several years to learn their skills.

CIVIL ENGINEER

Civil engineers design and build big structures, such as roads, bridges, and buildings. These are examples of **infrastructure**. There are different types of civil engineers. Some design the structures. Others help build them.

CIVIL ENGINEERING IS ONE OF THE OLDEST TYPES OF ENGINEERING.

Sometimes, civil engineers help design and build cities for people to live in. Civil engineers need to know about math, technology, and science. They need good planning and **communication** skills.

AEROSPACE ENGINEER

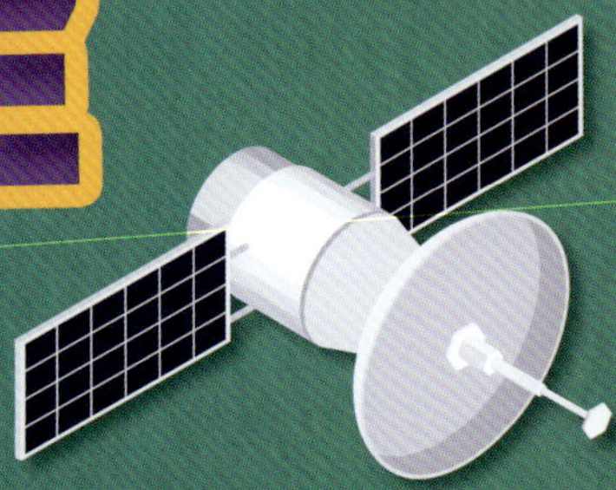

AERONAUTICAL ENGINEERS DESIGN AIRCRAFT BUT NOT SPACECRAFT.

Aerospace engineers design, build, and test aircraft. These include airplanes, spacecraft, and **satellites**. They build model aircraft using computers. Aerospace engineers make sure the aircraft they design are safe.

Some aerospace engineers are astronautical engineers. Astronautical engineers build machines that go into space. All aerospace engineers need math and science skills. They also need good planning skills and excellent attention to detail.

BE INSPIRED!

ASK QUESTIONS ABOUT HOW AIRCRAFT FLY.

ENVIRONMENTAL ENGINEER

Environmental engineers work on ways to protect the environment. They design ways to lower **pollution**. Environmental engineers figure out where pollution is coming from. They create plans to stop it from happening.

Environmental engineers might work with soil or in farming. They might help improve the ways people can recycle. Environmental engineers need knowledge of science. They also need good planning skills.

AUDIO ENGINEER

Audio engineers, or sound engineers, often work with musicians. They might work in a recording studio and record voices, music, or sound effects. Other audio engineers work at events, including concerts.

Audio engineers are in charge of the equipment they use to record sounds. They set up and control the equipment. Audio engineers need a good understanding of technology. They also need strong listening skills.

THE POWER OF STEAM

There are many amazing engineering careers in the world. We have looked at just a few of them. Engineering is an important field that can help make the world a better place.

BE INSPIRED!

STUDYING STEAM CAN CHANGE THE WORLD!

If you are excited by engineering, there are many incredible things you can do when you grow up. STEAM subjects can help you learn all the skills you need. It is important to work hard!

GLOSSARY

AFFORDABLE not costing too much

CAREER a job area that can be worked in for a large amount of a person's life

COMMUNICATION passing information between two or more things

DEVICES machines or inventions made to do something

ENVIRONMENTAL to do with the natural world

EQUIPMENT items that are needed to complete a certain job

INFRASTRUCTURE the things that a country needs to work properly, such as roads and bridges

POLLUTION harmful and dirty things that are added to an environment

PROSTHETIC LIMBS human-made replacements for arms and legs

SATELLITES machines in space that travel around planets, take photographs, and collect and send information

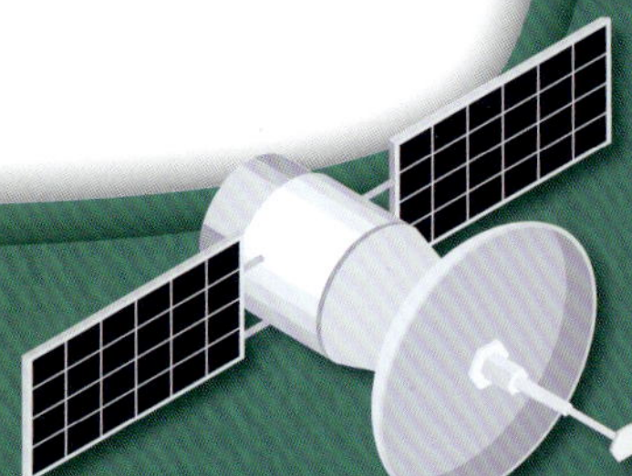

INDEX